Ridiculous Rhymes

The Essence Of Nonsense

Kaushik

pencil

ISBN 978-93-5610-867-7

Published in India 2022 by Pencil

A brand of
One Point Six Technologies Pvt. Ltd.
123, Building J2, Shram Seva Premises,
Wadala Truck Terminal, Wadala (E)
Mumbai 400037, Maharashtra, INDIA
E connect@thepencilapp.com
W www.thepencilapp.com

Author biography

The Interest Of The Author, Kaushik, In Literary Nonsense Was Aroused Quite Early When He Was Exposed To The Incredible Genius Of Late Sukumar Ray In Childhood. "Ridiculous Rhymes" Is The Author's Personal Tribute To The Brilliance Of The Legendary Sukumar Ray.

CONTENTS

Introduction

An Introduction To Late Sukumar Ray
(30 October, 1887 - 10 September, 1923)

Late Sukumar Ray Was A Legendary Bengali Poet, Story Writer And Playwright. As, Arguably, The Most Famous Indian Practitioner Of Literary Nonsense, He Is Often Compared To Lewis Carrol. His Works, Such As "Abol Tabol", "Ho Jo Bo Ro Lo", And "Pagla Dashu" Are Considered To Be Masterpieces Of Literary Nonsense, Equal In Stature To "Alice In Wonderland", And Regarded As Treasures Of Bengali Literature. Even Over More Than 90 Years After His Demise, Ray Still Continues To Remain As One Of The Most Popular Authors For Children, Both In West Bengal As Well As In Bangladesh.

The Soprano

Last Summer,
We Had Been Baffled By A Noise;
Which Had Emanated From The Voice,
Of Dharma Karma!

When Out Of The Blue,
We Had Heard Him Scream;
Over Mountain & Flowing Stream,
From Venice Down To Verona!

He Had Yelled,
As If His Own Life Were At Stake;
He Had Yelled,
As If It Were The End;

Panic Might Still Have Been Averted;
Had He Not Roared Like A Lion Thwarted!

The People Quite Amazed,
Had Retreated Rather Dazed;
Their Faces Had Turned Pale Very Swiftly!

They Had Beseeched Him,
"Mercy,
Dear Friend;

Our Endurance Is At An End,
Please Stop Singing Quickly!"

Terrified Puppies & Stunned Kittens,
Had Collapsed On The Wayside;

But Accursed Dharma,
Still As Stubborn As A Mule;
Had Refused To Halt His Lullaby!

The Beasts Had Resented The Blare,
From The Very First Moment;
They Had Heard It,
Astounded!

With Their Paws Up In The Air,
They Had Whined & Stared;
Or Wondered Quite Confounded!

We Had Protested Again,
But Quite In Vain;

"Will You Never Stop Singing?
Even Our Ears Are Ringing",

But His Voice Had Soared;
Out Of Our Reach,
In Spite Of How Much We Had Grumbled!

Even The Zephyr Had Wept,
On Hearing His Screech;
& Dilapidated Structures Had Crumbled,

Until;
In The Nick Of Time,
On The Scene Had Appeared An Old Goat;
Who Was Quite A Cranky Fellow!

He Had Cocked His Neck,
& Charged Ahead;
With Bellow Countering Bellow!

The Notes Of Chaos,
Were Sent For A Toss;
By The Music Of Blessed Violence,

As Dharma Finally Granted Us;
The Golden Gift Of Silence!

(Inspired By "Ganer Gunto" From "Abol Tabol" Composed By Late Sukumar Ray)

Scrambled

Not Only A Duck,
But A Porcupine As Well;
(Let Grammar Go To Hell),

Both Had Merged Into A 'Duckpine'!

"How?"
Only God Can Tell!

The Turtle Had Informed The Egret,
"It Is An Occasion For Celebration;
Since Remarkable Is Indeed,
Our 'Turtlegret' Incarnation!"

The Parrot Faced Chameleon,
Could Not Help But Worry;

"Will I Have To Now Forsake,
Insects For Green Chili?"

To Possess The Body Of The Scorpion,
The Goat Had Hatched A Conspiracy;
But Head & Torso Had Eventually Both,
Settled Amicably!

"I Am Tired Of Grazing On The Ground",
The Giraffe Had Heaved A Deep Sigh;

"With The Wings Of A Grasshopper,
If Only;
I Too Could Fly?!"

For The Antlers Of The Stag,
The Lion Had Entertained A Fascination;

Until The Moment,
His Wish Was Granted;
By A Curious Transformation!

The Cow Had Then Asked The Turkey,
Out Of Exasperation;

"Why Are You Stalking Me?"
Dreading Amalgamation!

The Whale & Elephant Had Still Remained,
A Formidable Combination;
As Long As Both Had Retained,
A Reciprocal Relation;

But When Jumbo Had Apprised The Orca,
Time To Retire To The Forest Was Nigh;
The Cretacean Had Enquired,
Heaving A Deep Sigh;

"Out Of The Water,
Won't I Die?"

(Inspired By "Khichuri" From "Abol Tabol" Composed By Late Sukumar Ray)

The Mystery Of The Missing Moustache

Our Boss Had Always Been A Genial Soul,
Who Had Seldom Lost His Temper;
Or Ordered Heads To Roll,

Which Was Why;
Nobody Had Expected,
Quite Such A Rigmarole;

Until The Day,
We Had Witnessed A Sinister Sight,

Which;
Ever Since Then,

On Every Dark Night Bereft Of Moonlight;
Still Compels Me To Writhe,
In Terrific Fright;

Since He Had Leapt Up Suddenly,
With Arms Wide Outstretched;
As He Was Feeling Rather Wretched!

He Had Suddenly Screamed Out,
With A Quake In His Call;

"Pick Me Up Quickly,
Before I Fall!"

The People Around,
Had Run Up & Down;
Searching For Any Cop,
Or Doctor Around!

"Pick Him Up With Caution.
He Might Bite!"

Had Warned A Colleague,
Who Was Not Too Bright;

Then We Had Heard A Preposterous Claim,
"My Moustache Has Been Stolen;
& You Are The Ones To Blame!"

A Moustache Heist Was Absurd!
His 'Tash Had Remained,
Where It Always Was!

Spluttering Like A Wafer,
While Being Fried Deep In Oil;
By Then His Blood Had Begun To Boil!

"Your Expressions Do Not Deceive Me,
I Know That You Are Slimy;
Since Your Moustaches Are Disgusting,
Nasty, Rotten, Lousy & Grimy!

If You Even Dare To Suggest,

This Moustache Is Mine;
Then Just Wait Until You Discover,
The Quantum Of Your Fine!"

While Scribbling Down In His Notepad,
Indictments & Fines;
With A Deep Sigh,
He Had Added A Few More Lines;

"These Scoundrels Are All Wicked & Vile!
If You Give Them An Inch,
Then They Try To Take A Mile!"

Scowling Away To Glory,
While Contemplating What To Do Next;
He Had Fumed,

"I Should Grab Their Whiskers,
& Smash Their Heads;
On The Teak Wood Desks!

A Moustache Is An Asset,
Which Can Neither Be Bought;
Nor Sold,
Since It Defines The Man;
Whether He Be Young Or Old!"

(Inspired By "Gonf Churi" From "Abol Tabol" Composed By Late Sukumar Ray)

The Eligible Bachelor

Although I Do Not Intend To Disparage,
But Just Recently Did I Learn;
Of Your Daughter's Impending Marriage!

If Stinky Sam Is Her Fiancé's Name,
Then Far & Wide Has Spread His Fame!

However,
His Complexion Is Rather Dark!
Although,
That Is Not His Fault;
Kindly Mark!

While His Appearance Is Not Too Foul,
His Face Does Resemble That Of An Owl!

"Academic Credentials?"
Now What Should I Say?

After Flunking Nineteen Times,
He Called It A Day!

"Financial Status?"
Quite Pathetic Indeed,
He Struggles To Make Both Ends Meet!

However,
His Family Is Not Too Bad;
Although,
His Brothers Are Slightly Mad!

One Is Quite Stubborn,
The Other Insane;
A Couple Of Rather Weird Men!

Wait,
I Almost Forgot About The Other Two!

They Are Absolute Gems,
Please Do Not Misconstrue!

One Is Quite Smart,
But Currently Residing In Prison;
For Forging Bank Notes,
Due To An Inexplicable Reason!

The Youngest Is A Drummer,
In A Foreign, Musical, Band;
Who Refuses To Return To His Own Motherland,

& Lest I Forget;
Stinky Sam Is Rather Meek,
Feeble, Sick & Extremely Weak!

However,
The Family Is Genuine Royalty;
As They Have Descended,
From King Lear's Dynasty!

Even The Hunch Back Of Notre Dame,
Is Related; By Blood, To Stinky Sam!

Anyway,
Since You Have Finally Selected;
Such An Eligible Bridegroom,
I Honestly Fail To Fathom;
The Reason For Your Sudden Gloom!

(Inspired By "Shot Patro" From "Abol Tabol" Composed By Late Sukumar Ray)

The Invention

Did You Know,
My Uncle Has Invented A Device;
Which,
Indeed;
Is A Sight For Sore Eyes?

Believe You Me,
Everybody Is Praising It To The Skies!

When Uncle Had Been Just A Toddler,
Or;
Perhaps,
Even Younger;

By Screaming Out,
"Pillage & Plunder":
In A Voice As Loud As Thunder,

He Had Struck Everybody;
Dumb With Wonder!

At An Age,
Others Are Barely Able To Enunciate;
"Mama",

The Unexpected Yell Had Generated;
An Acute Sensation Of Drama!

Everybody Had Then Predicted,
"If He Survives;
This Boy Will Alter Human Lives!"

Owing To A Contraption,
Which Motivates Everybody To Run;

Thereby,
Reducing A Five Hour Long Trip By Foot;
To Only One;

The Divine Will Has Finally Been Done,
With Destiny Eventually Earning;
It's Due Moment Under The Sun!

I Hereby Assert With Confidence,
Never Has Anything Been Invented;
Of Greater Significance!

What Initially Strikes The Beholder,
Is That It Must Be Strapped;
Onto The Shoulder!

To An Extended Arm,
Delicacies You Must Hook!
(The Sort Which You Can Either Buy,
Or Cook!)

The Choice Of Menu,

Depends Upon Your Predilections!
(Personally,
I Would Prefer Baked Confections!)

The Tempting Bait,
Induces The Urge To Eat;
Which,
In Turn;
Propels The Feet!

Since Your Mind Remains Intent On Eating,
You Can Not Help;
But Continue Speeding!

The Impact Of The Device Will Transform,
Our Entire Existence;
As We Will Sprint,
Notwithstanding The Distance!

For Granting Humanity,
Such An Invaluable Boon;
I Would Not Be Surprised,
If Uncle Were To Be Awarded;
Extremely Soon!

(Inspired By "Khuror Kol" From "Abol Tabol" Composed By Late Sukumar Ray)

Beware

What Are You Up To,
Big Wally?
Beware Of Exhaling So Loudly,
Since That Is Sheer Folly!

Were You Unaware That Last Year,
Right Next Door;
After Exhaling Loudly As Well,
Fred Had Collapsed On The Floor?

By Opening Your Mouth So Wide,
In The Process Of Heaving A Loud Sigh;
Do You Intend To Swallow,
Each & Every Insect, Spider & Fly?

You Had Better Walk Away Very Slowly,
Without Exerting Yourself Too Much;
Lest You End Up On A Crutch!

Glance Neither To Your Right,
Nor To Your Left,
Look Neither Behind,
Nor Ahead!

Did The Ancient Adage Not Suggest,

"Better A Thousand Times Careful;
Than Once Dead"?

What Was His Name?
Where Did He Dwell?

The Guy,
Who;
While Walking,
Fell Into A Well?

Wait A Second,
Lest I Forget;
Refrain From Ever Bathing In The Lake!

Encumbered By Such A Distended Body,
Wise Guy;
Should You Not Be Wary,
Of The Mishap Which Might Befall;
Were Anything To Go Awry?

If You Still Continue On Your Merry Way,
By Refusing To Listen To What I Say;
Then You Could Be Confronted By Fate,
& Might Soon Be Referred To As "Late"!

Why Are You Then So Upset,
Mate;
By What I Have Just Said,
When You Refuse To Control Your Weight?

Owing To Unhealthy Diet,

& Lack Of Exercise;
When The Reaper Grips You In His Vice,
Only Then Will You Wish;
You Had Heeded My Advice!

Jim Had Been A Smart Alec Too,
Always Overconfident;

Until The Moment,
Bang In The Middle Of The Road;
He Had Suddenly Met With An Accident!

(Inspired By "Shabdhan" From "Abol Tabol" Composed By Late Sukumar Ray)

The Pumpkin Bumpkin

If The Pumpkin Bumpkin Starts To Dance,
Then Pretend To Fall Into A Deep Trance!

If The Pumpkin Bumpkin Begins To Cry,
Then Heave A Deep Sigh;
& Lie Down Prone On The Floor,
As If You Were Just About To Die!

If The Pumpkin Bumpkin Starts To Roar,
Then Kneel Down Behind The Door;
While Reciting Homeric Verses,
With An Expression Quite Forlorn!

If The Pumpkin Bumpkin Begins To Run,
Then Turn Around To Aim At The Sun;
& Shoot It Down With A Pop Gun!

If The Pumpkin Bumpkin Wags Its Tail,
Then Set Sail;
On A Leaky Pail,
To Rescue A Whale;
From Drowning In The Gale,

But If You Dare To Scorn My Advice;
Or Consider It To Be Unwarranted,

By The Fury Of The Pumpkin Bumpkin;
Will You Then Be Confronted,

& When You Witness My Prophecy;
Fulfilled To The Letter,

Then Do Not Complain;
I Never Warned You,

Since It Was You;
Yourself,
Who Had Presumed That You Knew;
Your Own Business Much Better!

(Inspired By "Kumro Potash" From "Abol Tabol" Composed By Late Sukumar Ray)

The Rib-Tickling Fiend

Travel Wherever You Wish To,
My Friend,
Since Vacationing Is Now A Trend;
But Never Venture Anywhere Near,
The Rib-Tickling Fiend!

He Lurks Around The Corner,
In The Hope Of Snaring A Victim;
But Since His Residence Is Unknown,
It Is Impossible To Restrain Him!

His Modus Operandi Is Simple,
He Grabs You By The Sleeve;
& Relates Incredible Anecdotes,
Which He Expects You To Believe!

He Believes That His Stories Are Funny,
While Others Find Them Grim;
They Must Continue To Laugh Though,
If Only To Humour Him!

One Would Not Mind The Stories Much,
If They Were All That One Had To Bear;
But He Tickles You With A Feather As Well,
Which Is Hardly Fair!

Without Ceasing To Tickle,
He Continues To Cackle;

"Is It Not Quite Funny,
Pussy Cat Is Selling Horses' Eggs;
As Well As Fruit & Nuts & Honey?

The Eggs Are Black & Triangular,
While The Nuts Are Well Decorated;
The Fruit Are Adorned With Curlicues,
Quite Brilliantly Executed!

Pussy Cat Sings From Dawn To Dusk,
A String Of Weird Airs;

'Mew & Bray & Bark & Neigh',
But Pussy Claims That They Are Prayers!"

A Dangerous Maniac Is The Fiend,
For Even If You Have Had Enough;
He Will Not Cease Tickling Your Ribs,
Until You Begin To Laugh!

(Inspired By "Katu Kutu Buro" From "Abol Tabol" Composed By Late Sukumar Ray)

The Wobbly Shack Of The Old Hag

In A Dilapidated Shack,
Munching On A Snack;
Grins An Old Hag!

Wrapped In A Rug Replete With Cobwebs,
With Her Head Covered In Soot;
Hunches The Ancient Crone,
Whose Spine Is As Twisted As A Root!

She Staples The Crumbling Shack Together,
Then Sticks It Back With Glue!

Bleary Eyed,
With Needle & Thread;
She Stitches It Up Anew!

She Dare Not Lean On The Walls,
Lest The Pillars Crack!
She Dare Not Sneeze Too Loudly Either,
Lest She Knock Down The Wobbly Shack!

Whenever A Hawker Cries Out His Wares,
She Is Afraid That The Beams Might Break!
As Soon As Any Vehicle Honks Aloud,
The Foundation Proceeds To Shake!

Beneath A Ceiling Perforated By Leaks,
Respite From The Rain She Seeks;
But,
Despite However Much She Sweeps;
The Creaky, Old, Shack Still Squeaks!

Tirelessly,
Night & Day;
Amidst The Pervasive Decay,
She Wipes The Grime Away!

In Her Beloved, Own, Shack,
Behold The Toothless Grin;
Of The Decrepit, Old, Hag!

(Inspired By "Burir Bari" From "Abol Tabol" Composed By Late Sukumar Ray)

The Quack

Behold My Surgical Expertise,
As I Rid The World Of Disease!

"Practice Makes Perfect",
My Mentor Always Used To Say;

Hence,
I Operate On Dummies;
Night & Day!

What Cannot Be Attained By Enthusiasm?
What Can Diligence Not Achieve?

After Practising On Dummies Long Enough,
No Longer Does Surgery Appear As Tough!

The More That I Cut, Break Or Tear,
The More The Subject Grows Crystal Clear!

Decapitated Bodies,
Severed Limbs;
Detached Torsos In Abundance,
I Glue Them All Back Together Again!

No Scope Remains For Any Complacence,
Since I Am Ready To Treat Live Patients!

Bob,
Fetch A Few Sick Humans For Me;
& I Will Cure Them All In A Jiffy!

Sam,
Who Suffers From Corn's On His Feet;
Is The Ideal Patient For Me To Treat!

If You Can Trick Him Into Consulting Me,
I'll Excise His Corns;
With A Chain-Saw,
If Need Be!

Whosoever Is Suffering From Viral Fever,
All Those Suffer From Heart Ache;
Feel Free To Consult Me,
No Reason Exists At All To Be Afraid!

Why Is That Guy Limping?
Has He Fractured His Waist?
Drag Him Here,
& I Will Reset It Firmly With Paste!

Why Are You Crying?
Are Your Teeth Aching Again?
Let Me Pull Them Out With Pliers,
No Longer Will You Experience Any Pain!

Between Young & Old, Blind & Lame,
Deaf & Dumb Or Anorexic & Obese,
No Longer Do I Bother To Distinguish;

Since A Blow With A Hammer,
Is All That Is Required;
To Cure A Patient From Any Disease!

(Inspired By "Haature" From "Abol Tabol" Composed By Late Sukumar Ray)

Weird

Quite A Curious Creature,
Of Rather Dubious Breed;
Never Could Rest Contented,
Due To Insatiable Greed!

He Wailed Over The Meadows,
& Wept Into The Streams;
Plagued By Insatiable Ambition,
& Inexplicable Dreams!

Not Even For A Moment,
Did He Cease His Incessant Whine;
Forever Hoping Against Hope,
"I Wish That It Were Mine"!

He Desired A Voice,
Like The Cuckoo's Sweet Refrain;
Hence Practiced Day & Night,
But Warbled Quite In Vain!

He Envied The Birds,
As They Soared Up Into The Sky;
While Wishing That He Too Had Wings,
& Could Learn How To Fly!

Flaunting Its Trunk & Tusks,
He Could Perceive The Elephant Tread;
Why Then Should He Settle,
For Any Less On His Head?

He Saw The Kangaroo Hopping Along,
& Longed For His Own Legs;
To Be Lanky & Strong!

For The Lion's Proud Mane,
He Would Also Press Suit;
As Well As The Long, Scaly, Tail,
Of The Lizard To Boot!

He Coveted The Best From Nature,
Expecting Her To Fulfil All Of His Whims;
While Grumbling To Himself,
About His Own Inadequate Limbs;

Until,
Rather Unexpectedly;
On The 4th Of July,
He Was Suddenly Blessed With All;
He Had Ever Yearned To Try,

But Once The Excitement Was Over;
He Discovered,
To His Chagrin;
He Was Still Not In Clover!

What Would People Think,
If They Saw An Elephant Hop?

Could A Kangaroo Be Expected,
To Digest Banana Stalk?

If A Lion Roared Out "Cuckoo",
Would Anybody Be Rapt?
Would Either Trunk Or Tusks,
On A Kangaroo's Torso Be Apt?

What If People Jeered,
At A Jumbo That Flew;
& Boxed His Ears In Derision,
Or Even Flung At Him A Shoe?

What If They Ever Asked Him,
Right To His Face;

"Who Are You,
You Weirdo;
Nameless As Well As Homeless?"

What Would He Reply?
He Could Conjure Up No Defence!

At Long Last,
He Burst Out;
In Anguish Quite Intense,

"I Am Neither A Fish;
Nor A Frog,
I Am Not A Donkey;
Or Even A Dog,

I Am Neither A Moth;
Nor Butterfly,
I Am Not A Cake;
Or Even A Pie,

Woe Is Me;
Alas & Alack,

Who;
Then,
On Earth;
Exactly Am I?"

(Inspired By "Kimbhut" From "Abol Tabol" Composed By Late Sukumar Ray)

The Snack Thief

Whenever I Fall Asleep,
Prior To The Office Break;
My Lunch Disappears,
Invariably Before I Awake!

Tacos, Pizzas, Stroganoff,
A Succulent Steak…
No Less;

Pancakes, Plum Cake, Pudding,
& Only God Knows What Else!

The Food Mysteriously Vanishes,
In The Twinkling Of An Eye;

But Nobody Whom I Ask,
Is Able To Answer;
"Why?"

If I Were The Culprit,
However;
I Would Beware Of Tempting Fickle Fate,

Since Armed To The Teeth;
I Will Now Patiently Wait,
To Prevent The Crime;
Which HeI ntends To Perpetrate!

Tom, Dick, Harry,

Or Even The Mayor;
Reveal Your Identity,
If You Dare!

Although,
Whoever You Are;
I No Longer Care,
As You Are In;
For A Terrific Scare!

Just Wait & Watch,
You Shameless Hog;
I Will Hunt You Down,
Like A Rabid Dog!

If Again You Venture,
Anywhere Near;
Then Be Prepared To Render,
Your Final Prayer!"

(Inspired By "Chor Dhora" From "Abol Tabol" Composed By Late Sukumar Ray)

The Snake Charmer

Hi There,
Snake Charmer;

If You Have Any Serpents To Spare,
Would You Kindly Lend Me A Pair?

Those Which Can Neither Walk,
Nor Run;
& Would Never Harm Anyone?

Those Which Have Neither Fangs,
Nor Claws;
& Abide Strictly By The Laws?

Those Which Neither Hiss,
Nor Bite;
& Consume Only Milk & Rice?

Those Which Can Neither See,
Nor Hear;
& Cower Constantly In Mortal Fear?

I'll Tame Both Immediately,
If You Would Just Lend A Couple To Me!

(Inspired By "Baburam Shapure" From "Abol Tabol" Composed By Late Sukumar Ray)

The Concept

The Concept

Hey Sam,
Long Time;
No See!

I Will Explain That Concept To You,
If You Just Sit Down Beside Me!

Feverish,
Are You;
But Weren't You Just Screaming?

Do You Think That I Am Deaf,
& Do Not Know That You Are Lying?

So,
You Require A Doctor;
As Your Uncle Is Sick?!

Consult One Later,
Or I Will Prescribe A Drug Myself;
Which Will Enable Him To Tick,

But;

Come What May,
I Will Explain That Concept To You Today!

"Which Concept???"
Did You Forget It Already,
Or Drop It In The Sewer?

The Same Concept,
Which I Had Explained To You,
In Madame Bovary's Boudoir!

You Still Remember?!
That Is A Relief,
But Would Listening To It Again;
Cause Any Grief?

I Have Noticed,
You No Longer Drop In For A Cup Of Tea;
Is It Just My Imagination,
Or Have You Been Avoiding Me?

OK, Fine;
I Will Get On With It!
What Is The Tearing Hurry?

Can't You Wait Patiently,
Until I Collect My Thoughts;
While You Sit Quietly?

Hey,
Who Asked You To Sit?

Did You Expect Me To Fetch Those Books,
By My Own, Frail, Aged, Self;

Although You,
Yourself;
Still Remain So Young & Fit?

Cor, Blimey!
Whatever Possessed You,
To Retrieve The Dictionary?

Enough Is Enough,
Cease & Desist!

Please Stop Helping Me,
Before You Blow Up The Entire Quay!

Just Sit Down Quietly,
While I Order Some Pastry!

Anyway,
As I Was Explaining;

'Let Us Assume That A Miniscule Object,
Expanded Into A Colossus;

Or,
In Other Words,

The Core Of The Five Elements,
Remained Stuck In Reverse;

Then We Must Analyse,
The Source Of The Illusory Multiverse;

Or Imagine,
If You Will;

A Blade Of Grass,
On Which The Sun Is Shining Bright;

The Next Blade Is Illuminated,
However;
By A Shaft Of Moonlight!'

Why Are You Yawning?
Have You Even Been Listening?

What Did You Say?
"It Is Utter Nonsense"?!

Hadn't I Warned You Earlier,
To Grasp The Concept,
You Would Require Common Sense?

Can Anything Be Knocked,
Into A Brain Which Is Locked?

Hey,
Why Did You Suddenly Stand Up;
Even Before I Had Wound Up?

If You Were So Desperate To Flee,
Then Why Did You Come;

To Bother Me?

Nothing Ever Enters Your Ear,
How I Wish;
I Could Kick Your Rear?!

(Inspired By "Bujhiye Bola" From "Abol Tabol" Composed By Late Sukumar Ray)

The Greedy Glutton

Did The Greedy Glutton,
A Resident Of Bengal;
Break His Leg In A Nasty Fall,
From The Top Of A Lofty Wall;

Or Did His Uncle,
The Don Of The Opium Racket;
Quite Unexpectedly,
Kick The Bucket?

Why Else Would The Greedy Glutton,
A Connoisseur Of Mutton;
Lose His Daft Grin All Of A Sudden?

What Ails The Blighter?
Was He Stung By A Spider,
Or Did He Misplace His Cigar Lighter?

The Greedy Glutton Proceeds To Bawl,
"No;
Not At All!

I Had Been Happily Perched Atop A Wall,
Playing With My Favourite Doll;
When I Was Stumped,

By A Wicked Curve Ball!

If A Mosquito Settles Down,
On My Right;
Then With This Tail,
Will Its Existence I Blight!

If,
On The Left;
The Insect Dares To Bite,
Then My Other Tail Shall Mark;
Its Burial Site,

But If;
In The Exact Centre,
It Should Ever Alight;
Then With Which Tail,
Will The Pest I Fight?

If Only There Were No Moonlight Tonight,
Then I Would Weep Quite Brokenly;
At My Own Tragic Plight!

Two Tails Are All That I Have Got,
But More Than Only Two;
Unfortunately,
I Have Not!"

(Inspired By "Hunko Mukho Hangla" From "Abol Tabol"
Composed By Late Sukumar Ray)

The Law Of The Land

Curious Is The System Of A Country,
Which Shall Not Be Named;
Since For Sneezing Out Aloud,
Criminal Charges Might Be Framed!

If You Ever Fall Down,
While Strolling Down The Street;
Be Prepared To Be Hung Upside Down,
By The Toes Of Your Feet!

The Fine For Smiling Is Just A Smack,
On The Head;
With A Baseball Bat,
From An Immune Diplomat;

But The Penalty For Thinking,
Is Much Steeper Than That!

While Walking On The Way,
Your Feet Must Not Wander;
Since The Cops Will Rush In,
To Arrest You From Yonder;

But If You Even Attempt To Run,
You Will Be Forced To Stand For Hours;

Out In The Sun!

If You Ever Dare To Compose A Poem,
Then You Will Be Branded As Silly;
& Locked Up In Prison,
Until You Pay The Literary Fee;

But Is It Not The Very Last Straw,
If Snoring Is Deemed To Flout The Law?

(Inspired By "Ekushe Aain" From "Abol Tabol" Composed By Late Sukumar Ray)

The Bully

"Hey!
I Have Heard That You Said,
Yesterday;
White Was Red,

& Last Night At Three,
You Contrived To Snore;
Entirely Out Of Key,

& Each Morning;
You Screech & Howl,
Just Like A Demented, Paranoid, Fowl;

& None Of You,
I Saw When I Peered;
Ever Sports A Bushy Beard!

What Is Wrong With You,
You Stupid Lout?

I Shall Thrash You,
Until You Begin To Shout!

If Just Once,
I See You Glare;

Or Try My Patience,
If You Dare;

Or Once Again,
If I Hear You Bawl;
Just Like That,
For No Reason At All;

Then Do Not Expect Me,
To Desist From Violence;
Since I Have Mastered The Art,
Of Self-Defence!"

"Oh Well,
All Right;
Come & Fight,
Just Come & Fight!

You Know Not What You Are In For,
Mate;
But You'll Find Out Before It Is Too Late!"

"If Only My Uncle Were Present Here,
Then You Would Surely Quake In Fear!"

"Hit Me,
Will You?
You Had Better Stop,
Or Else I Will Summon The Nearest Cop!"

"Eh,
What Is That?

There Is No Reason To Be Rash!
Why Do We Not Talk Before We Clash?"

"Of Course,
That Is The Very Thing To Do!
You Know That I Would Never Bully You!

Now Let Us Bring This Quarrel To An End!
From Now On,
You Will Be My Dearest Friend!"

"Shake Hands,
Old Man,
It Is Time That I Went!

Do Not Take Offence,
When None Was Meant!"

"Bravo,
There Is A Sport;
So That Is All Right!

It Is Getting Late;
Good Night!"

(Inspired By "Narod Narod" From "Abol Tabol" Composed By Late Sukumar Ray)

The Cubs Of Monsieur Boo Hoo

Laughter Is Taboo,
For The Cubs Of Monsieur Boo Hoo!

"We Must Not Laugh",
They Wail;
Even After Hearing A Funny Tale!

They Cringe In Constant Fear,
Of Laughter;
Far Or Near!

They Start & Bound,
At Every Sound;
Apt To Convey Cheer!

With Their Peace Of Mind Forfeit,
They Continue;
By Rote,
To Repeat;

"We Prefer Genuine Grief,
Since Happiness Is A Cheat!"

They Keep An Anxious Eye,
On The Summer Sky;

For Any Sight Of Mirth,
Above The Earth;
Amidst The Cumuli!

The Darkness Of Night,
Provides No Respite;
Even As Feisty Fireflies In Flight,
Indulge In A Moonlit Dance Of Delight!

The Few Who Are Jolly,
& Consider Grief To Be Sheer Folly;
Must Not Deny The Hoos,
Their Right To Melancholy!

Monsieur Boo Hoo's Lair,
Stuffed With Gloom & Fear;
Is Doomed To Remain A Monument,
To Eternal Despair!

(Inspired By "Ram Gorurer Chhana" From "Abol Tabol" Composed By Late Sukumar Ray)

Spooky

On A Dark & Stormy Night,
Bereft Of Moonlight;
I Perceived,
Even Without My Spectacles;
A Strange & Sinister Sight!

Overcome By Dread,
Awfully Afraid;
I Could Discern A Couple Of Spectres,
Right Up Ahead!

I Could Not Help But Pray,
Since;
Neither Dared I Run Away,
Nor Dared I Stay;

However,
I Could Hear Quite Clearly;
Both Still Shrieking,
In Utmost Glee!

With Its Corrosive Voice,
The Infant Emitted A Shrill Noise;

But,

Concealed Behind A Lamp Post;
What Horrified Me The Most,
Were The Antics Of The "Momma" Ghost!

She Hurled A Brick At Her Son,
To Ascertain How Quickly He Could Run!

Dangling Him Upside-Down By The Hair,
She Urged Him To Somersault In The Air!

In An Ocean Of Despair,
Cowering In Mortal Fear;
I Watched Her Pummel Him,
& Box His Skeletal Ear!

Drenched By Incessant Rain,
I Overheard Her Whispered Refrain;

"My Life's Very Own Bane,
Only Source Of Pain;
& Future Scourge Of Men,

My Rat Faced Darling;
Dare You Threaten,
To Ever Cry Again?!"

Unexpectedly,
Out Of The Blue;
In Plain View,
She Flung At Him A Shoe!

"Why?"

I Have No Clue!

Thereafter,
In A Fit Of Rage;
She Locked Him Up In A Cage!

Suddenly,
In An Inexplicable Twist;
Both Apparitions Dissolved Into The Mist!

When I Next Ventured To Look,
I Could Perceive Only A Solitary Rook;
But Not Even A Single Spook!

(Inspired By "Bhuture Khela" From "Abol Tabol" Composed By Late Sukumar Ray)

The Astrologer

My Next-Door Neighbour Was Rollo,
Who Had Been The Jolliest Fellow!

Never Had I Met Anybody Else,
With A Personality Quite As Mellow!

Neither Had He Been Afflicted,
By Any Disease;
Nor Did His Mind Ever Lack Peace!

Filled To The Brim With Grace,
He Had Always Retained;
A Broad Smile On His Face!

Until The Day,
He Had Consulted;
An Astrologer In Bombay!

"Why?"
I Cannot Say,

But When He Returned From The Coast;
He Was Even Paler Than A Ghost!

While His Teeth Continued Chattering,

His Bones Never Ceased Rattling;
Nobody Knew What Was Wrong With Him,
The Situation Was Rather Baffling!

By Weeping Without Any Break,
He Had Grown As Thin As A Rake!

When We Asked Rollo,
Why He Was Crying;

He Commenced Whining,

"You Will Not Believe Me;
You Will Think That I Am Lying!

Woe Is Me,
Alas & Alack;
My Prospects Are Truly On The Rack!

My Future Is Quite Bleak,
As My Saturn Is Very Weak!

The Stars Have Aligned Against Me,
I Might As Well As Bid Farewell Already!

All This While,
Little Did I Realise;
The Universe Has Hatched A Conspiracy,
To Erase My Unwarranted Smile!

The Astrologer Has Predicted,
Unless I Fork Out The Requisite Bread;

I Shall Then Soon Be Dead!

I Must Placate,
With Expensive Gems & Jewels;
My Dark & Inexorable Fate!

From Where Will I,
Beg, Borrow Or Steal Enough Money;
To Avert My Own Dire Destiny?"

When We Had Next Met Rollo,
He Had Not Even Greeted Us With "Hello";

The Smile Had Been Absent,
As Had The Cheer;
Since,
No Longer;
Had He Still Remained A Jolly Fellow!

(Inspired By "Haath Gonona" From "Abol Tabol" Composed By Late Sukumar Ray)

An Essence Most Curious

Drowning Out The Clamour,
Of Bells & Gongs;
Vying In Vain For Attention,
The Deafening Roar Of Cannon;
Heralded The Royal Coronation!

While The Rest Of The Courtiers,
Arose To Cheer In Feudal Salutation;
The Faint Heart Of The Grand Vizier,
Palpitated In Grave Apprehension!

The King Then Asked The Grand Vizier,
Who Had Been Hiding Behind A Wall;

"Why Does Such An Awful Stench,
Pervade The Royal Court Hall?"

"Your Majesty,"
Protested The Grand Vizier;

"I Have Applied An Essence,
Which Is Not Abrasive At All!"

"Abrasive Or Not Shall Be Decided Later,
By William;

The Queen's Brother!"

"Dear Brother,"
The King Requested;

"If It Is Not Too Much Bother,
Then Will You Not Adjudicate;
On This Foul & Putrid Matter?"

"Royal Highness,"
Will Retorted;

"If Fratricide Is Your Intention,
Then Drown Me In The Stream;

But To Expect Me To Inhale,
An Odour So Obnoxious;
Is A Cruel,
& Rather Unusual Whim!"

Taken Quite Aback,
By The Unexpected Setback;
The King Then Requested Tiny Tim,
For An Honest Feedback!

Cursing Himself For Not Having Escaped,
Via The Rear Door;

Tiny Tim,
The Champion Wrestler;
Claimed That He Had Contracted Fever,
& Collapsed In A Heap On The Floor!

Pondered A Nonagenarian Nobleman,
Reputed To Be Quite Sly;

"I Have Nothing To Lose Even If I Try,
Since I Am Already Quite Old;
& Sooner Or Later,
All Of Us Must Die!

"Are You Cowards",
He Thundered;
"Not Ashamed,
Of Offering Excuses;
So Very Lame?

In The Service Of His Majesty,
I Am Willing To Endure Any Pain;
But Only If By Royal Decree,
A Reward I Might Hope To Claim!"

As Pleased As Punch,
The King Declared;

"Venerable Sir,
If You Accept The Challenge;
Then Your Valour Shall Not Be Futile,

Since The Reward Will Induce;
Any Mortal To Smile!"

The Courageous Courtier,
Then Proceeded With His Task;
To Sniff The Essence,

Without Even A Protective Mask!

From Headgear Up,
Right Down To The Cloak;
Not A Single Thread On The Grand Vizier,
Was Spared A Keen Examination;
By The Nostrils Of The Honest Bloke!

The Good Lord Was Praised,
By The Citizens Rather Amazed;

That The Old Sport,
Who Had Been Expected To Choke;
On The Pungent Smoke,
Still Did Not Croak!

(Inspired By "Gondho Bichaar" From "Abol Tabol" Composed By Late Sukumar Ray)

An Irresistible Invitation

Please Enter My Lair,
Without Any Fear;
& Accept My Hospitality,
If You Dare!

I Honestly Fail To Fathom Your Reluctance!
Are You Not Aware That I Abhor Violence?

Of The Inevitability Of My Defeat To You,
In The Event Of A Boxing Bout;
Could There Still Remain Any Doubt?

Is The Club In My Hand,
The Reason For Your Fright?

Do Not Worry,
For It Is Extremely Light!

If My Horns Scare You,
Then I Cannot Blame You;

Since You Are Entitled,
To Your Own Point Of View,
Even Though That Might Not Be True;

But I Wish That I Knew,
As I Still Do Not Have Any Clue;
Why I Would Ever Wish To Gore You!

While Dining On Guests Is Not Our Trait,
But You Should Still Not Tempt Fate;

Since If You Decline My Invitation,
Or Deny That My Assurances Are True;

Then Do Not Complain,
I Did Not Warn You;
When My Cubs Queue Up To Devour You!

(Inspired By "Bhoy Peo Na" From "Abol Tabol" Composed By Late Sukumar Ray)

The Cranky Cow

The Cranky Cow Is Not A Cow At All!
Actually,
It Is A Bird Instead!

Smartly Attired In A Fancy Suit,
It Has Never Been Spotted;
Without A Hat On Its Head!

Not Only Does It Have A Convoluted Tail,
But A Pair Of Twisted Horns As Well!

The Cranky Cow Has A Humongous Face,
With Drowsy Eyes!

Just Touch It Once,
& Watch How It Cries!

At The Slightest Sound,
It Startles Awake;
As Its Fragile Bones,
Begin To Quake!

If Subjected To Any Admonition,
The Cranky Cow Collapses;
In Nervous Trepidation!

Viewing Its Photograph Would Be Wise,
Since;
For An Adequate Description,
Even A Poem Might Not Suffice!

While Leaning Against The Wall,
The Cranky Cow Gasps For Breath;

Apparently,
On The Verge Of Death;

As If About To Bawl,
At Its Own, Tragic, Fate!

Neither Has Anybody Figured Out Yet,
What Prompts Its Sudden Fits Of Rage;
Or Why It Unexpectedly Loses Its Temper,

Nor Do We Still Know Quite Why;
It Frequently Collapses On The Floor,
& Then Proceeds To Pathetically Whimper!

It Strictly Abstains From Eggs & Meat,
It Avoids Rice As Well As Wheat!

Even If It Is Offered Fodder Or Seed,
It Still Stubbornly Refuses To Eat!

Its Diet Is Restricted To Soap & Wax,
Lest Its Memory Were Ever To Lapse!

Once,

It Had Swallowed A Dirty Rag;
Thereafter,
Its Health Had Begun To Flag!

If You Still Wish To Buy The Cranky Cow,
Mate;
Then I Might Sell It To You,
At A Reasonable Rate!

(Inspired By "Tnyash Goru" From "Abol Tabol" Composed By Late Sukumar Ray)

The Address

"Hey,
You There;
If It Is Not Too Much Trouble,
Then Could You Direct Me;
To The Residence Of Jack's Uncle?"

"Who Is Jack?"
"Whoa!

Then Jill,
At Least;
I Am Sure That You Must Know!

Jim Is Jill's Uncle,
Just For The Record!

John Is Jim's Son In Law,
Who Is Related To Jack;
Almost By The Umbilical Cord!"

"The Address?
Why Would I Not Tell You?
It Is Not Too Far Away From Park Avenue!

Go Straight Down The Road,

Keeping Your Eyes To The Right;
Until A Fork Appears In Your Sight!

Then You Must Crawl Along,
Through A Catacomb;
Singing A Sad Song,
Towards Saigon;

Until You Reach,
A Colossal Honeycomb!

If Then,
From There;
You Negotiate A Sharp Right,
Park Avenue Will Return To Your Sight!

Go Wherever You Want To From There,
Frankly;
I Do Not Care A Mite!"

(Inspired By “Thikana” From “Abol Tabol” Composed By Late Sukumar Ray)

Nice

Everything On Earth Is Nice!

You Are Nice
I Am Nice;

Dogs Are Nice,
Cats Are Nice;

Birds Are Nice,
Bees Are Nice;

Dancing In The Rain Is Nice,
Howling At The Moon Is Nice;

A Bald Head Shining In The Sun Is Nice,
A Pig-Tail Swaying In The Breeze Is Nice;

Hot Is Nice,
Cold Is Nice;

Dry Is Nice,
Wet Is Nice;

Pulao Is Nice,
Korma Is Nice;

Chicken Roasted On A Tandoor Is Nice,
Steak Sizzling On A Platter Is Nice;

Biryani Served With Raita Is Nice,
Fish Fried With Chips Is Nice;

Levantine Shwarma Is Nice,
Yorkshire Pudding Is Nice;

Bed Tea In The Morning Is Nice,
Strong Coffee After Dinner Is Nice;

Dunking A Dough Nut Into Milk Is Nice,
Even Smoking A Cuban Cigar Is Nice;

But Nothing Else Is Quite As Nice,
As Mom's Home Cooked Curry & Rice!

(Inspired By "Bhalo Re Bhalo" From "Abol Tabol" Composed By Late Sukumar Ray)
0-0-0

The Essence Of Nonsense

Come Ye Naive Fools,
To The Place Without Any Rules;
Explore Far Fetched Views,
Far Away From Schools!

Dreaming Away To Glory,
In A Whimsical Spree;
Come Whence Imagination,
Holds The Key!

Foot Loose & Fancy Free,
Come Dancing Merrily;
Banging On Your Drums In Glee!

Come To The Place Where Flowers Bloom,
Whilst Implausible Ballads Bards Croon;
Without Either Rhythm,
Or Tune;

Come To The Place,
Where Without A Trace;
The Mind Floats Away,
Like A Balloon!

Come All Of Ye Travellers,

To The World Of Babblers;
Come To The Place Devoid Of Time,
Swaying To The Beat Of Bizarre Rhyme!

Where Nothing Makes Any Sense,
To Those Who Are Dense;
Come To Discover The Essence,
Of Utter Nonsense!

(Inspired By "Abol Tabol" From "Abol Tabol" Composed By Late Sukumar Ray)